THE POTTER'S HANDS

Amber Onyeabor

Trilogy Christian Publishers
A Wholly Owned Subsidary of Trinity Broadcasting Network
2442 Michelle Drive
Tustin, CA 92780

For information, address Trilogy Christian Publishing
Rights Department, 2442 Michelle Drive, Tustin, CA 92780.
Trilogy Christian Publishing/ TBN and colophon are trademarks of Trinity Broadcasting Network.

For information about special discounts for bulk purchases, please contact Trilogy Christian Publishing.

Trilogy Disclaimer: The views and content expressed in this book are those of the author and may not necessarily reflect the views and doctrine of Trilogy Christian Publishing or the Trinity Broadcasting Network.

10 9 8 7 6 5 4 3 2 1

Library of Congress Cataloging-in-Publication Data is available.

ISBN 979-8-89333-418-0 (paperback)
ISBN 979-8-89333-419-7 (ebook)

This book is dedicated to my husband and children. Your unwavering support and encouragement made this book possible. You inspire me every day. I love you!

"Are you girls ready to go on our adventure?" asked Iah. Chi and Zi, Iah's sisters, followed behind him with Mommy. "It should be lots of fun!" Iah said. "We're going to learn about pottery today. I've never done pottery before, but Mommy says it's similar to playing with playdough, which I know we all love to do. I'm excited to learn more about pottery and to try it for myself," Iah explained.

1

"Oh look, it's Ruach!" exclaimed Chi.

"Hi, Ruach, are you joining us today?" asked Iah.

"Of course! Don't you know I'm always with you? Even when you don't see me!" Ruach answered.

"That's right," Iah said. "I forget about that sometimes."

2

"I heard you're going to learn about pottery today. God asked me to tag along, because there are some important things He'd like me to reveal to you kids," Ruach explained.

"Awesome! We get to learn about pottery and about God at the same time. I love it when that happens," said Iah excitedly.

Once the kids arrived at the pottery store, they stepped inside and saw the potter. He was sitting at his wheel, creating something. All kinds of creations surrounded him. He had various shapes, sizes, styles, and colors represented.

The potter looked up and said, "Hi, welcome! Please come closer so I can get you started on making something unique and beautiful."

"Have you thought about what you want to make yet?" asked the potter.

"I think I want to make a vase to put flowers in," said Chi.

"I haven't decided what I want to make yet," Iah said. "I either want to make a mug or a bowl. Can I think about it a little more?"

"Yes, but you can go ahead and get started. You can always change your mind while creating. That's one of the cool things about pottery," the potter answered.

"I hope he gives me some clay to play with."

The potter situated Iah and Chi in front of their own potter's wheels and gave them a slab of clay. He handed Zi a piece of clay while she sat in Mommy's lap, watching intently. The potter showed them how to use the wheel to make their own unique creations. He showed them how to manipulate the clay, how they can mold and shape the clay into whatever they'd like, and how they can change the shape of their design if they change their mind about what to make.

While the kids were busy creating, Ruach began to teach them how pottery relates to God. "I'm going to tell you a verse from the Bible," Ruach said. "Isaiah 64:8 (NKJV) says, 'But now, O Lord, You are our Father; We are the clay, and You our potter; And all we are the work of Your hand.'"

7

"That's interesting to think about, because no two people are exactly the same. When you make pottery by hand, you wouldn't be able to make two identical items," Iah pointed out.

"You're exactly right, Iah. Each person is different, and God is continually molding and shaping you into the image of His Son, Jesus Christ. You are always a work in progress," Ruach noted.

9

"Can you please explain more about that?" Chi asked. "I don't understand how we can always be a work in progress."

"Well, you are always growing! You may not be growing physically, but God is always seeking to use His Word to transform you from the inside out," Ruach answered. "God loves you so much and has a purpose and a plan for your life. But you need to trust Him. The clay can't spin on the wheel and shape itself, right?" Ruach inquired.

"Right. The clay wouldn't be able to do much on its own," the potter answered.

"See!" Ruach exclaimed. "You need to allow God to mold you. Surrender your life into His hands. When you give your life to God, He will always guide and lead you. He will mold you into who you are supposed to be, just like you're molding your clay into your desired creations."

"Thank you, Ruach! I definitely want to let God mold me," Chi said enthusiastically.

"Yes, me too! I've had so much fun learning how to do pottery and learning about how God is our potter," Iah said. "I finished molding my creation!"

"Me too!" Chi exclaimed.

"You're welcome. You know I'm always with you to help you learn more about God. He is proud of you for trusting Him to be your potter," Ruach said.

"I'm happy with how my vase turned out. I'm excited for it to be finished so I can put some flowers in it," Chi said.

"It looks beautiful, Chi!" Iah exclaimed. "I decided to make a mug. I think I will give it to Daddy once it's ready."

"You both did a wonderful job! I also appreciated hearing from Ruach today," the potter commented. "I'll finish drying and firing your creations for you, and I'll call you when they're ready to be picked up."

"Thank you!" Iah and Chi said in unison.

"Yes, thank you for teaching them about pottery!" Mommy said. "And thank you, Ruach, for teaching them more about God. Let's head home, kids!"

Everyone said goodbye, then Iah, Chi, and Zi headed home with Mommy. Ruach Hakodesh followed close behind.

"Bye, thank you!"

www.ingramcontent.com/pod-product-compliance
Lightning Source LLC
Chambersburg PA
CBHW081159050125
19943CB00012B/358